WAITING FOR The GREY MAN

A COLLECTION Of VERSES

S. VAN TOON

Waiting for the Grey Man: A Collection of Verses
©2021, S. Van Toon

ISBN: 978-1-66781-270-0

FOR ELAINE

MADMEN

We are the misunderstood monsters,

The space between molecules,

The bones of the brave in burnt-out capsules…

We float amongst the gutters, taking on the stains of your discarded lives,

We are the orphans of high society, the dull and spotted knives.

We are the humpbacked, walleyed, disappointments of entitlement,

The madmen who stand in the light of the sacrament,

And though you see us as a perilous shape,

To your acres of deadfalls and righteous red tape,

We shall float, so detached, above all of your snares,

Without fear, without fealty, free from all care…

We shall thrive—in the green mists of glorious madness,

A cleansing bleed in a festering abscess,

Observing the spiders devoured by their own broods,

A trembling id, setting fires with moods…

Now watch, as we sidestep your glamorous deadfalls,

To toast fire and absinthe in these hallowed halls…

Here, laughter is worth a thousand words,

As we soar out of sync, amongst lesser birds,

Because in the end, it's all a joke anyway…

Isn't that what you thought I would say?

So, would you rather be the punchline, or headline?

Toast to our suffering with a finely-matched wine?

I would rather be the joke—the teller of the tale,

Astride my own death, glorious and pale…

So let us lounge in fine detritus,

Watching this glorious apocalypse,

As she sways and grinds with heathen hips,

While the rest of the sane lose their manicured grips...

Now, close your eyes as the fire rains down,

Upon this broken, weary town,

And in this moment, you will see,

Just what it is like, to be someone like me...

Hold your breath, and feel yourself go,

To the worlds that I and my brethren know,

Past the fire and rain, the ice and snow,

To the place where the seeds of destruction grow...

And what's that I see? A smile, is it so?

Well, sit back my dear, and enjoy the show,

For it's better up here, than down there below,

Food for the serpents, maggots, and crows...

TELEPHONE

I tried to call you on the phone, just the other day,

You cut the line and burned my number—*guess you wanted it that way…*

I tried to call you, just to say my side of things you see,

Despite the fact you've never shown that much respect for me…

I tried to tell you that I cared, by letting you run the show—kneeling like a peasant in the freezing summer snow,

But you—in all your finery, your ego and outrage, you locked me like an animal, inside this orphan's cage…

You gifted me the courtesy of silence on your side—*I guess you thought you'd teach me that your rules I should abide…*

But here's the funny thing, my friend, the opposite occurred…

One day, your plan it flowered bright, and finally insured,

You've died inside my mind, my friend,

You've died inside my heart—*you saw to that, in all the ways you tore my life apart…*

Now, the only things remaining, are shadows of the past…

Blurry wallet sizes that are fading, oh, so fast.

So I had your funeral, buried you, and learned to live alone,

Then I cut the binds that joined us, and I smashed my telephone…

Your numbers gone, the pictures burned, the memories, a pyre,

Burning like the acid pain inside you helped inspire…

You tried to call me on the phone, lying on your bed,

But you forgot—the man upon the other side was dead.

URSA

We are friends, you and I.
You, a wall between myself and the monsters…
I burrow in your worn fibers,
I confide in your silent, glassy eyes.
I weep upon your lifeless body, that I have given soul and name.

We amble through watercolor fields, and soar over mountains,
Laughing at the perfection we feel…
I lean over the waters,
Slicing small currents with small hands as you take the wheel,
A tiny passenger—holding onto an idealized fantasy of father…

You were made by a sweaty, underpaid ant.
Factory pure they say—*I disagree*…
God made you,
In heaven—for me—to act as shield, sword, blanket and surrogate,
Armor-plated-dragon-slayer, mother-father and conduit.

When I am old, we will part ways in time,
As your body rests in a forgotten, dark place,
With my breath and tears, stained upon your face,
Steadily degrading, buttons loosening,
Glass eyes marred by time and neglect,
Covered in dust and curious insects…

Somewhere in that mess of fibers,

Is there a memory of a warm universe we shared?

When you were the only one that cared…

You cannot cry, but I can,

As only those who have lost, understand.

So thank you, friend,

For helping a child endure the long, terrible nights,

The deafening darkness and infinite slights,

The slow, grinding days,

And the loss of old ways…

For giving me a voice,

And ears to hear, arms to hold,

A shelter to sleep, in a kingdom gone cold…

Perhaps in the end, my life breathed some small measure into you?

For are you not as I see you? Imagine you?

I believed you into being…

And I know you were real, because so too, were the days,

And the feeling I had when we slumbered together,

A fortress of warmth and safety, in a house of storms.

So go to your rest,

And may it be,

Where children and angels roam wild and free…

And know, if there is indeed a spark within,

You will not be forgotten…

In the silence that keeps you.

WAITING FOR THE GREY MAN

My brain is burning…

A dike with a finger in it, chafed and bleeding,

Leaking, not speaking,

Reeking bile and dead fish piles…

A stink a mile high, for the King Fly.

It wasn't supposed to be this way

To a child reared on cathode ray specials, and comic book titans,

But lo and behold—I stare down the barrel of fate,

As a metal angel offers release, breathing death into my throat…

Almost took the plunge

But not this time.

There are still wounds to inflict,

And miles of skin for this killing world to feast upon…

I can take it

So they harden the soft infant to steel,

To be melted for the sweeps audience…

We are entertained.

The spirit quakes—like a shadow spitting poetry,

With a scarf in a dark corner of a neon abattoir…

Dare not confess my prayer for peace

Here, strength is weakness, and betas wear alpha masks.

Wolves linger, hungry for blood—*to distract from their own wounds,*

Hypocrites of the animal world…

These feet are blistered and burned,

Sandals worn flat—spit upon and spurned.

Too many miles and not enough smiles…

Can I withstand? To the end?

Be a friend and father—brother and saint?

I will look to my reasons—above and below,

And make a grim-eyed promise through flashing teeth,

To endure one more day—one more paranoid fantasy,

One more scar for the flesh diary…

For them I can take the monster's teeth.

I was born in fire anyway

Sure, it was only a cinder, but all things in time…

Now, the inferno blooms as charred armor falls away.

Grey man, can you hear me? See me burning?

Is your cloak large enough to hide me from my enemies?

A tent for storms and Judas brothers

Maybe I'll sit here a while—feeling your blade against my neck…

On the edge of release, on the tip of your tongue,

As a prayer for peace is answered…

With the long, grey sleep at last.

VERSUS

Once upon a time, there was a light in darkest nothing…
And this light, it knew somehow, someway, it was *becoming*.
It didn't know, it didn't care, how it came to be,
It just knew that it was real, and that it must be free…

It shined upon the darkness like a beacon in a storm,
It dreamed a thousand dreams, and took a thousand shining forms…
It split upon itself, so it could get a better view,
And gained a new perspective as it saw all things anew.

And with this truth, it blazed across the paths it laid before,
Of infinite creation, and the things it could adore…
It took two faces so the conversation would be fresh,
Then pierced the void with light—retracted—*this became its breath…*

It saw itself in every way that one can see a thing,
It wept the winter snow, and felt the warming of the spring,
It died a thousand times to see that death is just a dream,
Then raised itself from nothing, with a melancholy scream…

It made us both—and every thing that creeps and crawls or thinks,
It laid the sands in Egypt, and the stone that raised the Sphinx…
And now we sit upon the other side of this and joke,
While clouds arrange, and leaves blow strange on everlasting oak…

We laugh at fully-formed symphonic elder dreams,
Formed in nothingness before the pride of angels screamed…
We claim the sun—for in our eyes, its rays have clearly dawned,
This golden light among us, on all things it flames upon…

No matter that the light preceded all our hopes, my friend...
For in our folly, we believe this world is ours to bend.
While in the deepest dark, a voice calls sonorous and true,
Laughing at the things its lost and prideful children do.

FIGHT

The demon wants a fight...
But he's made a mistake in calculation,
For angels can be scary too, in retaliation.

Walking the thinnest of lines...
Finely-tuned control,
Divine rage...

Evil licks my boots at the river's edge,
Yet as I walk, goodness greets me with icy kisses in this furnace.
I clench my fist to welcome them...
(They think it will be an easy fight)
But they have not seen the likes of me
I am more than a suit of youth on a man's frame,
I am more than a scarred child in the dark...

So let us meet—claw for claw...
Give me your best,
And I promise you, I will give you mine...

You rise from the depths, to swallow me in dreams,
And I turn to face you, despite your machinations,
Apocalypse-eyed, megaton rage...
Fission, fusion, fury.

Your proxies will fall to the dust...
Then you will join them

For what were you ever at all?

A cowering shadow—tolerated by Heaven's brass.

Now, the rent is due, and the word has spoken…

I see fear in their eyes

And for a moment, they are as men.

I see the mask of pride fall,

As realization dawns—and somewhere, in the deepest darkness,

An alien fear scurries on insect legs, shaking the webs away.

Now, as the gears turn, and the numbers crunch to failure,

I hear you knocking on the door of no return…

Not so smug now

No more breathless rallies or golden thrones,

As the sycophants and seditionists return to the primordial shadows...

Back where they belong.

So prepare for the abyss you so revere, kingmaker,

For now, comes the hour of your unmasking...

And all the tyrant's toys cannot stem the tide,

As the waters reign down from the heights,

To drown your legions—far and wide…

We regret to inform you, sir:

It appears you've brought a knife to a GOD fight.

THE END

I am naked in the swirling black,

As the ache of reality pushes inwards upon blind eyes…

Stars form.

Now, the dream that was forgotten, returns—and I weep,

For my faith was not true,

And in the vast loneliness of my soul, I lost hope…

Yet now, with all things made clear, the vortex I offer myself to…

Its jaws cleanse the last residues of fear and doubt,

Scraping human remains away, harvesting the light of decades spent inspired and defeated…

And there, in the depths of my Father's hands, I understand the wonders before me…

And time was still.

I am falling—falling through a cylinder of spectrums…

Lights are meaning, and meaning has light.

I am a star—streaking through the black,

A laughing, weeping star…

And the universe is still.

I am home

Familiar voices soothe,

And a place prepared in the beginning, awaits…

I open the door to myself and walk in.

No truth is kept from me, for all things flow freely now,
A generous river—healing rain for a desert mind…
Now, I simply am—*and that is enough.*

And I was still at last.

THE GARDEN

In the ancient past, there was a boy who loved a queen…
And she, in the ways she could, loved the boy in return.
But soon, her nature bred an army, and the kingdom fell…

At dawn, the boy slept,
In strange rooms with stranger hosts,
Cruel and cold—and the sun did not shine…

The queen watched from her tower,
Satisfied the boy would endure…
And as his tears flowed, as the lashes stung his flesh,
She tended to her own gardens—leaving his to burn in the cold light of day.

And the kingdom fell.

By day, the boy walked in lonely halls—unloved and alone,
So he built for himself a high and terrible throne,
To keep the beasts at bay…
The queen watched still, seemingly unmoved,
As the boy stumbled, bled, and fell—crying out for mercy as the strangers broke
his spirit…

The boy grew angry, and forgot his light,
He wept by day, and screamed by night,
And the queen watched—gardens in bloom,
As her king beckoned her to gilded chambers…
And she chose to forget—for her pleasures were many.

And the kingdom fell.

Night came, and the boy was now a man,
As the queen returned to claim him triumphantly,
Spreading legend across the hills,
Of how she saved the boy from his enemies…

By field, forest, and sea, she sang their praises,
Taking the man on many adventures…
But the distance between them was vast,
And the wounds still bled—overtaking the banquets and glamour,
Smearing filth upon fine linen—piercing the night with their
anguish, unforgiven…
And the tides rose, as walls of ice swelled and crashed,
All things swallowed by their past…

Now, war was in the air…
And soon, the cannons would flame once more,
As her legions marched, shaking the earth.
And the queen, in that hour of doom, left the man—for he was a mirror,
Whose dread she dare not face…

Dawn came at last, and the man was now old and frail,
His queen, long dead…
He now, a curved and bent form, scraping the earth,
With broken gait and dimmed hope—a shadow of its former shade.
What a story, they would say…
Who would choose to end this way?

And a specter fell upon her court then—eyes burned white,
Yet still discerning the faint color of her dying gardens,
Their bloom now in full and magnificent decay...
Surrounding her bones and those of her king.

The color of their merriment wreathed still, those halls…
The smell of flushed skin and wine, the ring of laughter,
O'er countless nights of peace and contentment.
While just beyond the well-tended courtyards and stout gates,
Past the vast measures of her dominion, in the low country,
He waited—*for her to return…*

But that was long ago.

And so, in the fading of his hours,
He entertained a small lie…
To ward off the chill of the grave, the cold sorrows of his heart.
He imagined his birthright had somehow been honored in this ruin…
No, it was not a lie!

They could not deny the sun,
For it shines
They can not deny the wind,
For it howls through these very halls!

Now, after the passing of an age,
He too, would not be denied.
For he saw himself in her mirror, and was indeed, real…
In the court of his birth,
The promise of a future standing in stone.

And so, an old man remembered being a prince,

Straightening himself up with a weary smile,

For he was now, the last soul standing…

Victorious it seemed.

Now, at the passing of shades,

He had bested his captors at last…

Endured their insults, taunts, and blows,

And he did not succumb, did not yield,

For he had become both sword and shield…

But then, the smile fell,

For this was no victory!

To stand among the bones of kin,

And see what might have been…

And he wept for lost years,

For the garden was a beautiful fiction—to occupy her time—instead of him.

In the end, she simply could not love,

Could not keep the promises she made…

And all that was left, was broken stone—a court in ruin, an empty throne,

And he to watch—as night returned,

While all the kingdom, slowly burned.

In time, he would fall to the earth,

To nourish the dying flowers of a once-shining courtyard…

And perhaps by that end, their bones may lie together in peace.

Now, in this grim silence,

A final measure of kindness—a weary prayer answered...

For in this place of ghosts, a single rose blooms from the dark,

Nourished by the memories of a love below.

And somewhere, beyond broken hearts and loss,

Where better angels soar free of their burdens,

They will watch the first rains nourish her garden...

As a single flower stands—strong and true—rising from the pain of ages.

THE HERO

The Hero stands in the cold night air,
Tears cutting jagged memories down his face.
Failure in the face of beauty, nervous jitters willing out…
Too much to approach—so he watches her from a distance.
Someday he will overcome.

The worm turns,
Feeds the bird…
Teaches it humility—nutrient-rich heartache.

The Hero watches them dance,
Standing alone—a jester amongst lesser fools,
King of an empty court…
Youth darts like errant bullets, deflecting their own exclusion,
And he waits—among the refuse of the refused.

The Hero bides his time, for someday will be his day…
He will ride—upon a belching beast of steel and pop culture,
Leather-suited, convoluted,
Easy to read for those that speak the language…
That of daydreams and dime-store heroes.

The Hero heads home,
Parents waiting in four-wheeled embarrassment.

The Hero smiles, as lights bid goodbye,
Reminders of moments lost…

Stars doused in guarded sadness now,
Hiding the dreams his heart won't allow…
The universe is closed: Open at six.
Thank you for your business!

The Hero sleeps—content to rest,
To love and fight another day…
For there will be other dances, other beauties,
Other fairs, blades to cross,
Songs to sing, and tights to wash.
Someday, the Jester will be king,
And his subjects will kindly forget,
That once, he was a small, stained squire,
Strutting awkwardly through the footprints of noblemen…
Just another fool in a bustling square,
Prancing about without a care.

Yet, when the sun shines down upon him,
Among the small who masquerade as giants,
A future crown falls in shadow upon the morning dew,
Showing his quality.

NOW HIRING

God and I had a conversation...

It was fairly one sided—he spoke, I understood.

He showed me his true face, and as the light cascaded across mine,

A divine disco ball spun the music of spheres.

It seems the beat was always there,

I just forgot to put my ears to the earth...

But like elephants, I remember everything now.

Illumination—an underground chain letter,

Easily lost in the junk mail of things...

But no worries,

For he told me the puzzle would complete itself one day,

That things were working out...

Even he seemed surprised.

I saw his plan:

An Art Deco truth—a postmodern scripture sculpture in a trendy boutique,

Waited on by unintended elitists, and poorly-trained translation agents,

Secretly paid by dark energies, to bend what was once a straight road.

Look at them all...

Bored retail slaves and bitter ex-queens of the fair,

Suitors dried up, promises broken, and crowns stiff with mothballs...

Someone has to feed the jackals,

And the sadness is sweet and plenty.

Burning cars on a midnight shoulder, diamonds on a reaper's bones,

Glittering collections of nick-nacks made to distract…

The universal truck stop waitress…

Sweet in the center, but chewy outside.

Love is candy—sweet, cheap, and disposable…

Some tastes better than others,

So we sample to sort it out.

Some flavors are subtle—most are lost in cast-iron minds…

I'm a rare vintage, most would say!

Doubtful.

So, some fast,

Some slow, but steady…

See? The world moves for the turtle,

Out of sheer respect.

And these brave few

May they find peace on mysterious islands,

Spending their days in the fading sun together,

Last of their kind,

Outmoded by bigger shells, to hide from hares…

Slow virtue pushed aside for speedy lies.

So we watched it all

Ever shifting…

"Soon, they will know," he said, and his time would be done.

He asked if I needed a job

No need for money here,

Pay me in something else…

Truth? Is there a bank for that?

Call my agent, he'll work the deal.

I said I would think about it

So we did lunch—and he told me he regretted mosquitos…

I told him that was big of him,

Which was funny, because he's surprisingly short…

So we talked, and he laughed,

The sound of a vibrating violin string,

The wobble of a warped stand-up bass,

Punished by a repressed, sweaty hero with lightning in his loins…

The blue works well with the flaming sword

I would buy your stuff…

Problem is, will the world?

Can we market holiness? Aren't we already?

As the fleas run the dog pound, the wolves shake their heads,

Serving sweet irony on dulled silver to rusted robots.

And I looked then, through a gilded, golden glass,

Below to a teeming mass…

All the soap in the world can't wash that guilt away

Clean? A temporary state…

Souls are chalkboards anyway,

Erase it, sure,

But the last words endure,

Smudges of fear and delight…

Pleasure becomes pain in the long run anyway.

Perfection is boring,

So let's practice on ourselves…

If we fall enough, perhaps we'll write in a straight line…

This is the way of things

We will laugh about this later as men,

And as men, we will cry for our lost youth,

Just like the rest of them…

For happiness is a slippery fish in greasepaint hands.

Vaudeville would love us,

The saddest show of all…

Four stars is quite dark when you think about it

So perhaps one more?

Then I can see you better to judge!

But before the unpleasantries,

Let us reminisce

I remember like you do…

First day of school: (didn't like each other much)

Now, we are friends

You saw my first knocks, picked me up…

We made this suit together

A temporary tuxedo for the last emperor…

Got to give it credit,

It's hard to hold all that human-ness.

But that's the way it rumbles, when your foundations crumble,

Sweaty heads and palms—clammy clams in a cold grocery tank,

Surrounded by cold shoulders, nose to crumpled paper,

Oblivious to our crustacean dreams of escape…

Foreplay for a frigid mistress.

So we sit—exposed, waiting to boil…

Wait—I can have your mercy, or your vengeance?

I'll take door number one, and dump the hot water while you're at it…

But back to the show…

I pick an ant out of the static,

Will it be madman? Tyrant or addict?

Pain tattooed on a baby's flesh…

Destiny.

Oh, it's coming…

Cherubic sponges, carrying seas of suffering

Just wait—it's quiet now, but it's gonna get loud!

The house will bend, sideways tears in a shrieking wind,

Wash away the grime

Dirty thoughts and dirty ideas, played out between dirty people on an ivory stage,

How can they keep a straight face?

Spectators share the burden

Don't get too close, these lost animals spit…

Stained? More like blessed,

To watch the folly of children…

Down they go

Reach in, pick them up, dust them off…

Divine alchemy.

Deserts become oceans when superheated,

And like us, the braver specks push their way forward into boulders,

Some to crush the smaller ones, some to block the wind for others…

I had seen enough…

Exhausted, but eager to help.

Time to stop bitching and pitch in

So I took the job.

God said thank you in his usual way

So I read the magazines in the lobby: recipes to die for,

How to please your ex with sex, but not love…

Like a child loves a bee, or a bike that makes him feel like the wind.

I was ready now

What else could I say? He's my father after all…

Don't like to see him sad.

I can chip in—mow the lawn,

Fix some things…

Why not?

He left me some numbers…

In case of emergency—or act of, well, you know who—

And a memo:

"If we can love, we are saved."

It's funny, because for once I actually understood what he was talking about…

So down I go,

To the hot center of things,

To join my friends,

To lift them from the mud,

To cry with them…

And as we hold each other,

Tightly now,

Smile—for who else do we have, but each other?

SPIDERS AND FLIES

The spider wore lipstick…
The fly was tempted.
He said she was beautiful…
She made an exception.

They spoke at arm's length—silk twisting in the moonlight,
A thousand faces in his eyes, all beautiful…
She saw his qualities with less
As he drew closer, lust overtook her,
Dripping poison and mating lubricant…
He didn't care—nothing would top this
A kiss…and the world shook…

The fly spoke, and the spider listened…
But soon, it was clear her ears were not tuned to his voice.
The fly continued—frustrated and compassionate,
Sorrow and joy spilling from his lips…
But she heard only silence.
He was earnest—she was too,
But still—a gulf no wings could traverse…
Wind streaked through antennae, as he beheld her,
Like a starlet in a silent film, cigarette burns and all…
Animal cinema—Oscars for aphids.

"Insects can smile…
For I saw a spider do just such a thing once,"
The old fly said to his offspring.
Nobody believed him,

But he smiled anyway, wings thumping like a heartbeat in love,

Remembering their parting—a kaleidoscope of contradictions...

And then he flew away...

Because she let him

Grateful for moments shared...

And thus, he watched both his life and death,

Pivot away on silk, as the poison took new meaning for him...

A slow strain to darken hearts in time.

A spider loved a fly once...

Enough to starve for a day,

Feasting on sweet regret instead.

Romance lost on lost roads,

Dreaming of where he might go,

As their warm tether stretched and snapped,

While she sat—thin and grey,

Smiling at gentle mercies and nervous conversation...

As the long sleep took her.

And he felt something lost then—in his easy chair,

As the golden light of dusk took him too...

Elemental amnesia,

Pierced by unrequited affections,

As they meet once more—jitters and smiles in an undying place...

Spider and Fly.

1989

In a darkened carnival of extortion,
I gleefully surrender my lunch money…
To wield a sword—*and slay a dragon.*

So many deaths, so little time…
Marching forward in steel fatigues,
To cleanse Detroit of 2-D villainy,
I leap cool as an '80s action cop,
Above a sea of hobos packing mystery needles.
My fiery helmet and leather vest, twin fashion statements,
As I skip from one flaming fever dream to the next…
Insert coin to continue

Standing on a floor of neon Christmas-sweater nausea,
With worn out British Knights, to save lost damsels,
I take another inch, with each life,
Until the boss comes with fire-breathing bluster,
And code designed to steal fortunes from angry boys who won't give up…

I love it here:
Here in the tinkling, clinking, beeping and banging,
Of flippers and chutes, and carefully-machined routes to glory…
Here, we brag over half-crushed juice boxes, and the bones of Hinoxes,
Through sweat and dirt—*on the battlefields of youth…*

And now, you're gone—replaced by mainstream simplicity,
Dumbed-down dumbbells smashing through barriers,
Only to create new ones…

And all that is left, where you once stood, is a place to buy candles,
Or a thousand different kinds of basketball shoes,
In colors that would make an LSD blotter sick…
What a shame.

But we remember
Those who graced your hallowed halls,
To become tiny men through blood, sweat, and tears…
Here, we learned to never give up,
To concentrate like Jedi Masters…
Twitch, flinch, dodge, and parry,
Showing us monsters weren't that scary…
Well, a little bit, because that's the fun,
As we played until our time was done…

Thank you, dear friend…
Thank you for teaching us, that any beast can be overcome,
With time—*and enough quarters.*

MAKING FRIENDS WITH WOLVES

The shark and I had lunch today…
Thankfully, it was not me.
He told me they don't usually court their food…
I appreciated the sentiment
Said it was hard work being a killer—corporate layoffs at sea,
A pink slipstream of chum and failure, as far as the eye can see.
Said the cages served no purpose,
That they could get us if they wanted to.

He was fascinated by our own fascination
Tiny scientists in a sea of false hypotheses,
Sacrificial lambs on a spring breeze…

So why me? Was it something I said?
Why can't we both just sit and break bread?
He thought for a moment, then grinned jagged steel,
Never thought I'd be arguing with a prospective meal
But, there's always a first—so let me explain…
I don't crave your fear, anguish, or pain,
I just do as I must, and you're here in the way,
So I will be predator—and you must be prey…

But do you hate your wine?
Resent your soup?
No—just a machine like me,
So lay off the guilt and set yourself free…
You do what you must—as I will for now,
But we can be friends if the ocean allows…

He turned thoughtful then, profile in shade…

This is the world in which we are made

Even sharks worry…

That's why we never stop moving,

Sleep? For the dead—so we just keep grooving…

And he smiled again, but kindly this time,

Sending a shiver up this old spine,

For those eyes of his had seen many wars,

And blood in the tides of many great shores…

And the sadness within, was clear then to see,

As he floated in silence, looking at me…

Same time next week?

Weather and mood in the air…

But I promise to give you a start that is fair,

So bring your cage, just in case,

Your legs get tired and you lose the race,

I'd hate to devour you just to save face,

So let us all pray for a sliver of grace…

So—a stay of execution from a waiting tomb,

As my razor guest glides beyond the gloom,

An endless canvas of mournful grey,

As I live to breathe another day…

See, even hares can dine with lions,
Said a wise man once, a noble scion,
Everyone learns something—nobody dies,
As the sun sets and the gull cries…

Now, the ocean retains its native blue,
As I hold my breath, and make my way through…
Peace on these tides—if only for today,
Lamb and wolf—predator and prey.

STARVING ARTIST

The skies are quiet...
But inside, within the cloud,
A fierce, hidden thunder.

For all the world, sunny skies...
But alone, an inky landscape.
Vast brushes of midnight, muscle, and rage.
This is the dream factory...
Always open.

Now hiring dedicated neurons
Cells divide, sharing ideas...
Too much noise—can't sleep,
Inspiration elusive, talk is cheap.
The higher mind pilots...
I obey.

Sit down and write some more
The only true audience, self-satisfaction
Does anyone truly understand?
As the sparks fly—the gears grind?
Faded efficiencies convey thoughts,
Thoughts and primal words...
A rush up the spine, as invisible fireworks burst,
Silent—but explosive just the same...
Just ask the painter
He'll tell you all about it,
As brushes speak volumes unsaid in polite society.

Listen to us

For you need us to save you when things grow dark,

With our torrents and currents of storm and color,

Of sound and fury…

Tales of warning and woe,

To a cynical world that bends a beggar's ear to be whole again…

Your ships sail for jagged stone—disguised as idealized dreams,

While we swim in these depths, immune to the siren's venom…

A gift of pain—and from it, flows the truths you seek…

We do not want your coin, your rapturous rafters, or your tin idols,

For we are compensated in different ways…

The storm feeds us generously

And we are whole.

So listen to us—and perhaps you can soar above the jaws and shadows,

That brought these tales to you—*the darkness we know so well.*

And you shall step upon our backs once more,

Over these dark depths,

As we mine the jewels that light your way.

But as you look down, upon our fell travels,

Know that some men were born to stand in fire,

As others are consumed by it.

WATER

Look at me go...
Bobbing in circles, cold and pissed off,
Still fighting the same currents.

This river has personality
It says hello by punching me in the face...
But I can barely feel, so I refuse to kneel,
As I dig into its sides with a giddy squeal,
And with broken heart and pickled liver,
I fire every last arrow in my quiver...
This amuses the river.

So I've got this boat...
Wasn't made by me, but I'll use it just the same.
One of a kind: chips, dents, and stains tell a story...
Don't know if she's seaworthy,
But I wouldn't trade her for all the tea in China, and a billion cups.

Think or swim
Not a lisp, a motto.

So, I threw the paddles overboard...
It's better this way.
Don't hit bottom,
There's things down there, natural and unnatural...
Both have teeth
So don't dwell in cobwebbed corners,

For curious is a barking spider waiting for cats,

And satisfaction won't cut it on this web.

But back to my boat

I'm sailing to the island of misfits…

Square holes and round thoughts,

A different set of eyes for a crooked world.

Everyone else sees straight lines…

I think I'll pass on the correction.

So tell me the truth—because ignorance is not bliss,

As I float in this river—cold, but happy…

Almost there

If we want it bad enough, we'll survive the drop…

So hold my hand as we go,

Gravity reversed—tiny tears racing to meet us,

As cold, airy breath howls a song of fear and wonder…

Almost there

Freezing…

There's the light—head for it!

And we'll ride this tide with eyes wide,

Ignoring the dread and doubt inside,

For when this is over, we'll remember again,

And maybe, just maybe, they'll consider us men…

Let us rest now—in this tide pool of fools,

Lashed by the sting of mortality, punch-drunk from the foam of this loam.

If you could spare a kindness, *cheer on the others*

Those dark forms swirling in the same cauldron as we…

Look at them go!

Lend them your battle song

And if there be no more use for your blade,

Hurl it swift to those churning shapes,

For you of all warriors, know the odds of escape.

There—now comes a few—rising above the knives below,

Where eyeless monsters soar and glow,

To face the dread waters in which we dwell…

Wish them your own victories—wish them well.

BEAST

The beast is sleeping—guard your step,
He's sure to wake, you see…
See how he breathes—with newfound ease,
Free from ferocity.

Free for now,
Of thunderbolts and iron hammer falls,
Of moonlit dreams, and midnight screams,
And blood upon the walls…

The vampire's mark is absent from his pale flesh tonight,
As the demons share a cigarette, beneath the moon so bright.
Behold the beast—a child at peace, from waking chloroform,
Where fire, hate, and anguish whip a scarred and broken form…

In dreams, he longs for mother—softly held from all his fear,
And for father's strength—to heal his wounds and hold him near.
He longs for lover's hair, and flowered sweat upon her chin,
He longs to find a cause, where he can finally buy in…
To howl and dance and thump and drink,
The brotherhood of life,
To laugh and sing and weep and dodge, the reaper's poisoned knife…

The beast, he dreams of worlds beyond,
This scarred and cankered sore,
The beast, he dreams of heights that fall from grace, forevermore.

So kiss his brow, and hear the deep and low breath from his breast,

Hold his shaking form, and place your cheek upon his chest...

For in this beast, we see a child—asleep in dreams serene,

As gentle mother comes, to claim her infant as a queen...

BLOOD

I cut to bleed the hate I feel,

I cut to feel the pain,

I cut because my weakness is a frightened fucking stain...

I cut the hero's mark upon my face in fraud and fear,

I cut the jagged scars upon this mask to trace the tears...

I cut to feel the grey like foxes, neutered of their blades,

I cut to bleed in sleep, like Ronin in their prouder days.

I cut to feed the hatred of these dark sins that I bear,

I cut to burn the blue away, the youth and golden hair...

And when the lines firm up, and all the scars become complete,

I'll walk the earth a paper doll—a torn and tattered sheet.

For every stroke of art, must find its root in pain, you see...

And in the end, this scarred remorse is all I'm sure to be.

So off I go—a vaporous phantom,

Skulking in the night,

Dwelling in this filth,

Because it makes me feel so right.

In love with tragedy, (my own)

Soap operas for the flies...

Soaring in the last remains of long-forgotten skies.

FRANCES

A roman candle with diaper rash and a hurricane's wrath,
A miracle that walks, drools, and grins,
Now my face hurts from smiling, as my insides spin…

You throw yourself on the floor,
To tickle our mutual sense of comedy.
You give me purpose and courage,
And armor to fend off tragedy.
Fierce conviction, benediction—a mountain armed with an axe,
To crush any interloper.
Dread be to he who comes with ill intent and bad hair,
To betray the heart of my maiden fair,
For the ogre smells the blood of the insect he once was…
Did you hear that, cuz?
For my golem is awake and standing guard,
As you nervously pace in my front yard…
And it warns with red eyes, to settle all scores,
To crush, smash, and leave steaming on the floor,
The bones of pimple-faced paramours…

But not yet…
For those days are far ahead,
So I put away my tears and dread,
As your scent calms me.
Now, eyes express tides that mouths cannot speak,
As your hands enfold mine, and I weep,
For our chains are divine—our foundations deep.

You are a gift

From the highest seat, to the lowest fool,

A ray of peace amongst hours, cold and cruel,

A thunderbolt—tiny, yet quite effective,

And all I want, is to be strong and good—*heroic, protective.*

Your joy splinters growth rings,

Explodes long-standing oak in a shower of '80s pyrotechnics,

As we chuckle together at the absurdity of fear…

My blazing cherub—so precious and dear.

I love you so

You love me back

For even the sun shines upon the faithful worm,

If he endures the cold earth upon his knees,

For enough ages of pain and disdain,

As the pillars fall and the seas drain,

For underneath it all, a seed of hope,

As the worm twists on the end of its rope…

Now, she reaches out with her golden hand,

For she sees far, and understands.

She severs the twists of pain and fury,

That ensnare the beast, the rancor and worry…

And he falls into her waiting arms at last,

Free for this hour, from an orphan's past.

Who'd have thought we'd get this far?
Under darkened skies, with endless scars,
This light we hold—it's what we are,
Shining a path from a jar...
And you—my angel, you shine at night,
Setting all bones and wrongs right...

What a road it has been
What a weary climb
What a pair we are—what a strange, grand time.

FLIGHTLESS BIRDS

Let's go flying
I'll run, you hold your breath…
See? We can't die here, it's only in my mind.
My wings work, do yours?
It's a start I guess…

After a moment, the sickness passes…
Are we actually moving?
Birds are overrated…
Oh look, the eagle is offended,
Someone offer him a hairpiece,
For he *is* bald after all…
Overcompensating
I guess that explains the tattoos…
All that rippling, ruffled feathers, and staged screaming,
He looks exhausted.

"Can't we just fly like normal people?" she asked.
We would, but we lost our wings,
For we were too afraid to keep them.
So better to keep things grounded,
Solid footing, solid earth,
Low altitudes and self-worth…
Ironic for those that dream of flight.

Upside down on a falling star, on a black sheet of ice,

An expiration date for a discount head-trip,

And I'm all out of nice…

We're melting baby, but oh—what beautiful wickedness…

Foiled by goodness at last,

As we sink—black bow, sails, and mast.

We are a shoebox presentation for a bored classroom of snot-nosed bumpkins,

Counting the slow click of the clock, itching to take off,

Racing for home, for sitcoms and stroganoff.

But we're already flying

Didn't you know?

Or have you lost your sense of the wind?

The illusion of stillness betrays us…

A million hapless fliers—looking to join hands,

As the ground rushes to meet-and-greet,

To the sound of a leering, jeering, marching band.

Better yet? *Let's be still instead*

Let us not be afraid to face the silence in our heads…

Wouldn't that be a rush?

So, what are we afraid of?

To find ourselves in a world without senses?

Free to wander without chains or fences?

Here, there is still a you and me,

Past well-practiced masks,

And social pretenses…

Here, where we float in the darkness,

Without limb or sound,

No horizon, no ground,

Just stretching acres free of predetermination.

Pure mind on loop

Better get used to it…

Because there's only one flavor to this soup.

So take my hand,

It's time to fly…

And once the old drafts return, lifting us higher than before,

You'll wonder why you were ever afraid at all.

HOLLYWOOD

There's a dragon dressed like a man,
And he's guarding my money...
I ask him if we can share?
He says it's not in the budget
Color by committee, paint for numbers...
I say I can improve the place
My aim is true, my motives clean,
Snow falling onto an oil slick,
A false-god machine...

I have visions!
We have plenty
I have ideas!
We steal those
I have skill!
So do carpenters.
Fully staffed by bean-counting frauds,
Oozing with green and shiny greed,
Overgrown kids gorging on weeds,
Guarding the fortress of ineptitude,
Inspiring decay and decrepitude.
Holding court over the bottom line,
A panel of asses, sheep, and swine.

Ears refusing to hear,
While complaining of deafness...
Eyes claiming blindness,
Leaving visions to die,

Stacked in a mailroom, twenty feet high...

The slavish worship of form over truth,

Just look at those beautiful margins!

What cost a dream?

What price rapture?

We'll fix it in post

With a thousand toys,

That handicap talented good girls and boys...

Overseas, ancillary, spin-off, reboot!

Don't ever let a good lie get in the way of the truth!

Money is made to burn,

So start the bonfires and raise the corpses,

For another dead horse on parade!

Let's tell this joke until it's funny again for the wrong reasons,

As we scorch the sky, and complain of lost seasons.

The science of ever-lessoning returns...

Broken arms patting pampered backs, feeding diamonds to worms.

Who would choose dead art over living dreams?

I tell him he's making a mistake

He smiles behind his broken gate,

Tied to his masters and a miserable fate.

See, his batteries are low,

And his log files are showing,

As the nuclear fire they set keeps on glowing,

Rotting the apples from the inside out,

As they distract with kickbacks—preen, and pout.

So much for sci-fi

As I bicker with my lo-fi host,

A copy of a copy of a dead man's ghost.

But he hears my pitch!

Genres are dead…

The people don't want originality,

It's far too much reality!

After all, it's better to settle into that cozy death plunge,

Hooked to the IV of nostalgia,

As fear becomes a security blanket that smothers us all.

"Ideas are dead," he says…

Mined from broken hills, under mountains purged of inspiration,

An eden drained dry of childlike creations.

See, yours will be forgotten in time,

As the world will forget you…

But don't feel bad, you're not unique!

You can't afford this chic boutique!

It's status, baby!

Hits, clicks, impressions, depression,

Come over to my home studio for a session!

We'll hire a team of the worst to write the best song you ever heard!

Nothing like the best grease to polish a turd,

Into a fugazi…

That the world, unknowing in its complacency,

Will hoist aloft like a holy prophecy.

I have a hunch we'll do lunch

See you on the 32nd!

Maybe there's something for you in the mailroom...

And just like that, the door slams with a final NO,

Of ringing steel and humiliation...

So much for this calling—this so-called vocation.

So I pick up my guts from the sidewalk and leave,

To find a dark hole and quietly grieve...

I feel sorry for him

At least I still have my eyes,

As the world opens once more before me.

Don't like the road? Change the color...

Maybe yellow brick—that's the trick!

He would rather stay on the ground—behind a gate, in a box,

Safe and stolen

A fossil from a darker age, locked within a liar's cage,

Soon to be tread upon by revolutionaries that were once called madmen.

Me?

I'll keep trying,

Because on this stage, I've always been dying!

So what's to fear?

Low domestic gross?

We'll sell cereal and socks from coast-to-coast...

And another NO won't change my story,

Like Indy, I'm hunting for fortune and glory,

And if the fire and fangs don't get me,

Your cynicism sure as hell won't affect me,

Because there's more than one rainbow,

And the dragons call to me…

For if I can walk the long dark, and slay your kind,

I'm sure to see my name on a neon sign,

And you can park my car on that glorious day,

When your grosses shrivel up and blow away…

My pen is a sword, a shield,

A hero in a sun-kissed field,

Anything I choose,

A bluff, a turn, a clever ruse…

I see in color now

Bleed and sweat,

To carve these titans from the ashes and tears of the past,

And when they stand at last, we will stride these landscapes toward their city of thieves,

To shatter the gates, as the stories that *must* be told,

Warm a weary world in the midnight cold…

And they will see the light on that glorious day,

When their pillars of smoke shudder and sway…

Oh, look—somebody slayed the dragon at last!

He was old and greedy, feeble and fat,

He ate too much and couldn't fight back,

As the unsung heroes pressed their attack.

And now, we'll sing songs of the low man today,

As we stand upon its grave and dance away…

Then I took the money he'd stolen from me,

And gave it to a kid to write his own story.

But I hear a voice in the rubble and ruin
Call my attorney, and let's get suin'!
We'll rebuild this Babylon brick by brick!
We'll show those peasants some shiny, new tricks!
Our stories will heal the old and the sick!
And we'll build a new beast, with scales ten feet thick...
They'll never assault our gates again,
For we'll ready our swords and the legal pen...

And this will be our legacy...
For the low man can never be set free.

So I did the only sensible thing:
I dropped a big rock on that cancerous king,
And that was the end of the dragon you see,
And now it's just you, an idea, and me.
And you can decide if it moves your soul,
As we take back this world, take back control,
For dreams, they are priceless, can't you see?
So let's talk a producing and writing fee...
I'll need good suits, applause, and fresh adulation...
How else am I supposed to find inspiration?

YOUTH

The window dims…
Dusk falls upon fragrant grass,
Steps of youth in eons past,
When joy was not so hard to grasp,
As breezes set us each in flight,
From roaring dawn, to silent night.

We dreamed as future men in freedom…
But look what we have become
Pale shadows of our heroic selves,
With books of dreams, stored sour on fading shelves.

What shook us from our course?
The waves? The tides? The wind?
How do we rebuild the road?
How do we start again?

My mind is full to bursting,
Leaking worry, sorrow, pain…
And all I see is darkness, and a cold, relentless rain.
I'm trapped in steel springs of thought,
Fenced in by this hate…
Could our younger minds have dreamed up such a cruel and tragic fate?

The inner dialogue has too long been antithetical…
Now as I walk, upon my head, a tweaked-out reaper's reticle.
Not enough sleep

Swollen glands and ancient plans of who will fall below,

A three-ring mushroom cloud at a flea-market peepshow.

Itchy fingers ready to pull out the final stop,

The hand that cuts the ribbon for the opening of shop...

Will you take my heart? Sullen, twisted, low?

Will you take my soul and all that I will ever know?

I guess the only thing to do, is dig deep in the mud,

To fight and slash at every beast who comes to claim this blood.

But there were promises, assurances, fairy tales,

High castles, jeweled crowns, and rippling sails...

Promises of adventure, love, and piracy,

Glamour, laughter, lunacy!

The fictions of a generalized stamp set,

Marked upon the foreheads of a gullible army of children.

But that is over now

As greying eyes see the grim light of dawn,

And the graves of dreamers on the endless hillside beyond.

So let us share a tear

For the castle is dust,

Along with love and mercy, family and trust.

The king and queen, they're dead...

And here I stand, with only memories in my head.

Perhaps we can warm each other by this fire?

Fueled by snapshots of better times...

Content to share the same pain as we share this bitter flame.

Yes, let us shelter in the shadow of this monolith,

A dream too big to be realized,

Now, a barrier against the sting of the wind,

In this place of forgetting…

Yet, I smile with you by my side,

For it takes one to know one,

And our eyes have seen the dying of a once-glorious age,

As we scuttle and scrape for scraps in this cage…

Here, we will share this silent, final dawn,

As the canvases burn, by the graves of pawns.

These banners smolder with steely dignity now,

The last they can muster…

Like proud matrons, fixing a crooked corset,

In a tavern of sweaty brutes intent on taking what is not theirs.

Here, foolish hopes are laid to final rest,

As we cling adrift, above unknown depths,

Soon to be our resting place.

But look on the bright side dear…

Perhaps when the currents pull at our bones,

We will know a gentle touch at last…

And when the moon washes over us, in the shallows of the forgotten,

Another pair of eyes will see the glimmering we never could.

PRAYER FOR THE LIVING

For every killer, I see an infant that lost its way,
Screaming in a carnival of flashing lights,
And shrieking hammer bells…
Every scream, a plea for self-preservation in a careless world,
Of isolated islands—each as uninhabitable as the next.

This—a place of barbed thoughts and open wounds,
Infinite potential—yet predictable failure…
Small variations in a pattern of lost souls
I seek to understand myself through you…
I love you, for I know your pain,
I have lived both of ours, again and again,
For I am connected to all things,
And bear all burdens beside you,
As the armies of darkness push violently through…

Once, I slept in the darkness—before your time,
Alone in the crushing abyss,
Before light, before a willing pierced the infinite obsidian,
With a proud and joyful fury…
A still point of madness—seeking to understand how it came to be…
And you saved me from this wretched loneliness—heard my terrible plea.

And so, the world will never know how my heart breaks…
At your despair, your dark and desperate hours,
Failures and broken dreams,
Shattered hearts and animal screams…
For I love you all

Even as you strike one another—curse, blade, and bullet,

Imprison, gag, defile and bind,

Headlong to the deepest darkness,

Where you shall always find, that the void is unsustainable...

As I did.

You see, malice is a self-defeating army,

In the flush of crimson war rituals...

All raging breath and war-drum heartbeats,

Ragged grist beneath thundering feet...

Pride and suicide in a world incomplete.

Yet, perhaps, after the demons have torn us apart,

We'll find at last, our gentle hearts.

For every lost cause, I weep...

For lonely ends without friends,

Gun in mouth and blade to wrist,

Oh, how you struggled to exist...

This life of ten thousand exposed nerve endings,

Of aching, naked, bones on display,

Before a colosseum of fools, who clamor and bray,

Brave children, I love you—tomorrow and today.

I feel your pain as you fall below the tides of night,

And long to release you from it...

But a promise was made, and muscle only grows in acid-flame,

As wisdom blossoms through crushing stone,

The only way it can—naked and alone...

A courageous antennae, swaying in the breeze of giant footfalls,

Awaiting its end beneath an indifferent sky.

We must both feel this fire

This lonely burn of separation,

To one day taste the bliss of light...

Floating like careless specks of mystery matter on a warm breeze,

We shall be—surrounded by the love you have always known,

Through me

All sides must be seen to understand the endless road...

So forgive me, as I forgive you,

On this dusty lane, content to be still and dream,

For the bliss of home that was always waiting.

STILL LIFE

I remember the day we were together
Avatars on a canvas of false memories,
The walking dead in a spring breeze…

I wanted to include you,
Even though you make me feel bad about myself.
It's odd we return to the beast to be bitten…
Stimulation games for tired flesh
What else can I do? It's boring here…
Make a fire? Watch a movie?
The adults will party upstairs in heaven,
While the children burn in the basement.

It takes a certain kind of winter to create steam,
As the sword is drawn from the ice,
Stronger than before…
Its edges sharp enough to cut a whisper in two.

All of our glorious tongues of fall,
Now made insignificant aerosol…
Aloft beside legions of heartbroken dust,
That were once men, who others could trust.

When I grow up, I want to be a child...

You, will still be old

Some people are born that way...

Wish things could have been different

Try to remember the good things...

Were there any at all?

But we can pretend, like that painting of yours...

I was the kid in white—you wore red,

As the trees swayed peacefully above our heads.

And so, we feast on this daily bread,

The left behind—and the long-since dead.

DEATH IS A STATE OF MIND

There's a secret only I know,
And it's not a good one
Soon, I will be checking out:
One way—keep the baggage, there's plenty.

No need for a mid-flight beverage,
Or windows,
The clouds are my landscape…
I trim and angle with soaring hands,
Each breath of rain released to form anew…
Light dances from my shape—ruby fire,
Golden pain, and purple strain.
I am a jester and professor—measure and calm,
Calamity pleasured…

We made a pact once
And I guess I forgot…
But like the good friends they are,
They will remind me with 90 mph of steel.
These friends of mine...

Tough love is not tough…
A facsimile printed on brass knuckles,
Leather straps, and tough guy belt buckles.
Some help with a kiss or extended hands,
These guys bring a hearse and a marching band.

Now, they remove my eyes on a place atop the sun,

Breakfast on a supernova—brunches with blackholes…

Isn't this fun?

Cocktails with saints—afterparties with angels,

And somewhere along the edge, I see into space,

So far below—wondering how far each one will go…

The shadows of lost fish,

Swimming dully towards the light,

Flicking and straining with all of their might…

And when the man comes,

With his heralds and drums,

They will sit beside me,

Finally free.

FIRSTBORN

In the dawn I watched you,

Emerge as a miracle…

Fresh to this world,

Full of promise,

A clean slate.

Helpless, I held you,

Clothed you,

Nourished you,

Lifted you high…

So light—eyes aglow with wonder.

We danced and I wept, dreaming with dread of a future,

Of us upon a cursed floor,

The years lost behind us,

And only I to guard these memories…

To hold them as they slip between my fingers.

You are grown now…

Not complete, but in progress,

And I cannot recognize you

No less loved, in fact more,

But as my love grows, so too, does my fear…

Of losing you.

And should we be fortunate to share many years together,

The best we can hope for, is you at my side,

As I step where none can return…

Hoping against hope there is a light waiting,

And not the oblivion of all we hold dear...

Praying and weeping I will see you again,

In some unknown place of mystery,

To hold you against me…

In peace and paradise

Wouldn't that be nice?

Remembering the small hours together...

Home was there, and here too.

The only difference is the long walk we have shared,

As the bonds that join us, grow thick with rust and desperation.

I will hold to you now, even if the abyss takes me,

And know, that as the pillars that guard my treasures of you fall,

The last thing I will see, will be a man holding his child…

In heaven on earth.

OCEAN

There she goes again
Through the spirit made physical...
Through the blue dream of eldritch mystery.
Swimming with titans,
Dispelling myths,
Shattering stereotypes and hysteria...
With steely composure and arcing fins.

They must recognize her,
For the forms differ—but the inner language is the same...
I'm okay if you're okay
A cautious ballet frozen in time,
Coursing through nightmare waters,
And sweat-drenched dreams...
Making them sublime and still.

Opening the curtain, the inner light spills through,
Sending away garish monsters made by human hands,
Revealing the old ones—content to soar upon an endless dreamscape.
She joins them—revealing the true form of the beast,
Wise and removed—*deadly if provoked or disrespected...*
Yet content to glide in the mystery with mere mortals,
In a place free of knives and angles.
Here, we are formless—opposing perspectives,
Free of the sting of hurled invective...

So what is left for us? Just the sharing of time and space,

And the infinite dream…

What a gift it is to soar beside you,

As I feel something ancient and true,

In these many, wondrous shades of blue.

THE BAT

The city is dark,
Wet—full of shadows and neon.
The ghosts of old pains haunt these tenements,
Prayers unheard before indifferent monuments…
Stained concrete tells a story,
The end of dreams of triumph and glory.

Into this shadow, you enter…
A boy in a suit of armor,
Lost in time—offering a rose to the departed…
When the heavens fell, and worlds shattered,
And you lost the only ones who mattered.

In the stillness of the expanse,
You found purpose
In the toil of your bones,
You found power
A symbol of your darkest hour…
Now, strides the beast within,
A golem forged to trample sin.

Soaring on midnight skies,
Above animal fear and desperate cries,
Raining down fire from heaven,
To hold back the darkness—if only for a moment…

An angel forged of gunmetal and talons,

Prowling this wicked garden, for the scent of lesser beasts,

For only one can carry this mantle—a crown of blood and tears.

Each night the same...

Different victims,

Different names,

All to send homage to the dead,

As you battle the inferno inside your head.

Now, you see with new sight,

As the shadow draws you into the night,

Here—you are no longer small,

No longer afraid to fall,

For you already have—and you'll never stop,

You are judge, jury, and crooked cop...

So look to the moon, as it welcomes you bright,

For here, you are master, warrior,

KNIGHT.

ORPHAN

Once, I was a child,

Passing through the current,

Into the flow,

Churned and chopped,

Spit out,

Rolling in the red tides below...

Decades would be spent repairing those wounds.

Now, I am a man,

Betting the farm on a jester's plan…

My mind, a coiled spring,

That prays for release,

From the jaws of a bored and spoiled beast.

Chemical fires burn…

Acrid, acid, alkaline, ache,

How I wish for sleep when I awake…

Like Atlas, holding up the pillars of sanity,

Driven to endure by mortal vanity,

Slowly sinking into the soil,

As the waters within come to a boil...

I push back against them all

The shadows and voices and vices,

A failed fixer in a moment of crisis,

And I pray for that occasional glimpse,

Into green fields and white towers,

Sun-dappled waters and forgotten flowers…

There, I remember what it is to be free…

To be me

Now, I sink back into myself,

Losing the memory of it all…

And as the hot springs below,

Beckon me to give up, to let go,

I soldier on…

Tendons quaking, bones shaking,

Through burning fields of my own making…

Yet, I keep an eye on the rains beyond,

As I claw my way to paradise…

It's all I have—this dream of mine,

I can taste it, smell it, drink it like wine…

There, I reach with new limbs, see with new vision,

As the stones fall from this bastard's prison…

Tear down the walls, melt the steel,

To reveal the endless golden fields,

That were always there beneath it…

And so, when words become walls,

And thoughts curve space and time,

From what is, to what should not be,

That is where you will find me…

Guilty of imagined crimes

A senile child, tottering down a baking sidewalk,

Old before my time,

Crawling from the sea with an unfused spine…

The cell doors are open…

Yet I sit, blind to my freedom,

Forgetting I am sitting at all,

As I carve these bent figures upon the wall…

Sleep used to be an escape

A reset button for an overheated processor…

Now, the fear of deep, dark places,

Takes the rest I have earned,

And these hard-won graces.

So I watch as the hours pass,

A chalk outline in broken glass…

Each day, I awake anew,

Soul black-and-blue,

Unrested, heavy mind,

Fog and mist, the ties that bind.

Thoughts perpetually dancing,

On the tip of an infinite tongue,

Wishing for time lost—*while restless and young…*

The problem is, we all look the same from the outside…

Invisible worlds explode within,

As heroes fight to hold up fraying timbers,

Dashing from infernos, children in hand,

Across a charred and cursed land.

The remains of innocence, kept behind ever-weakening walls,

Piercing the night with a siren's call…

This is what you have wrought:

A child obliterated under the onslaught,

Of hands and words, volume, control,

Kept alone in a foul, loathsome hole,

Now to emerge—*the unkempt beast,*

That walks the hills of this sleeping village…

When I am gone, they will say:

He was a monster

Forgetting who sewed the bodies together,

And poured the lightning down,

Awakening something terrible in this clean and quiet town…

Now, at last, with eyes closed like a child,

I return to the shadows—unformed and wild,

To safe, dark places, far and wide,

Here, I will slumber—slumber and hide.

MARRIAGE

No one tells you how it actually is
No tactics can avail,
As the trenches are dug,
And the gate-smashers rumble forward…
See the pitch flame to life!

Weaned on sitcom laugh tracks,
Prom queens and snow-capped quarterbacks,
High school sweethearts,
And ships that never drift apart,
We enter the race, sure to win,
Assuming our better half will give in…

Then comes the fireworks—the bombs and brigades,
Sirens screaming, tears streaming,
Late-night curses, promises and vows,
Riding high in hearses, look at us now…
Fast to the grave.

And we stand with each other,
Hurling bolts from self-righteous Olympus…
Blinding, scarring, smashing the bedrock
We've spent years tending,
The fences we've been mending,
Only to do it again, in blind repetition…
What a glorious vision.

Is this love?

Layers falling to the ground,

Acid-flame scarred and unbound...

Friendship, once a shining steward of this town,

Now, a stained chalk form upon unkept grounds.

We have stricken one another...struck, ducked, and covered,

Forming something new and terrible—where once was something old and pure...

Chasing other shiny lures.

A sculptor's blade trims idealized youth,

To reveal grim age.

And what is beneath? In the heart of the watcher?

A raised and lone statue in the square,

Who speaks of tears and joy, laughter and despair...

He says:

When the war is finally over, and we stand upon these fields of ash,

Call it victory to find within, a lone, standing timber,

A single, shining core...

Forgetting the barbs, wounds, and storms,

The broken promises, and shattered norms...

Remember! The fierce tides that brought you here,

The fallout and fear!

These waves have struck and crashed upon us,

Smoothing our ragged edges,

Into the unbroken seed.

This lone survivor—a teller of woes and warfare,

Who braved the terrible heights others would not dare…

Forged unbreakable, unmistakable,

Immersed in countless days of darkness,

And crushing currents deep…

Cleansed of the dreams of youth,

Where old wounds fester and creep...

Now, let us be gentle and familiar,

Humble and broken,

Ready to repair one another,

With these vows we have spoken...

Let us hold each other now

Surviving ourselves…

Living to see this final dawn,

And the fields we once doted on…

This is love—the old ones said,

Yet those not ready to learn, passed the words in stone,

Unhearing, unseeing, and alone…

In time, all will live by this

All who seek to pass beyond fairy tales,

And angry gales,

Into this blissful womb…

So let us walk the long road once more,
To see what the hours have in store.
Here, where we drew bitter steel,
And fell on countless battlefields...

Now, at the end, we may rest,
Having passed this final test...
To share in this terrible silence,
Free from these memories of violence...

Returning to what we once were now,
Wars at an end, ego committed to ash,
Accepting the selves we have become...
Together.

A STATE OF GEORGIA

You patient fortress
You, who endures the icy breath of night,
And smiles the same…
A shadow of my former self,
A vapor of this flame.
Now, in this arena,
Surrounded by iron fools,
Red tape and low man's rules,
You rise into being...

Again, you come…
The self that will not be denied
See how they pillaged! See how they tried!
Can I face the nearly drowned?
As you wear this gleaming crown?

Your smile endures my raging spirit,
Acid words and crushing volumes,
Cursed portraits and stained heirlooms…
And you laugh throughout,
Cutting the storm to size,
With a wink of those golden, knowing eyes…

This fire will aid you in time…
And those who know your light,
Will warm cold hands around your essence,
While the rest huddle close to lesser fires,
Unable to see the splendid shapes you cast upon the stone.

What a gift you are!

And what a monster I have become…

To forget my own mark,

And the hands who burned this brand upon you…

Yet if I could only remember,

To join you in the bliss that surrounds me,

The peace that confounds me,

As I slash and flail, and howl this plea,

A wounded beast—forgetting he is free…

Now, you take this cold form with ease,

A cooling rain on a fiery breeze…

Your eyes, like fireworks to a lost soldier, on his knees,

Celebrating the end of separation,

And the death of wars, inside and out…

You—you who shall return us home,

The home that holds these wounds together.

What a gift to know you

My simple foolery,

Your subtle charm…

Georgia my dear

LADY OF SWORDS

You, who shares this flame,

You, who I cannot face...

In primal days, I learned to hate this face,

And resent yours.

The tragedy is, the water left undisturbed,

Would have adored the vessels on its wake...

You, who fascinates and transcends me,

In physical feats and mental cheats,

Your fire barely contained...

In spring you bloom,

And by winter, you burn once again,

Oblivious to the rules of shared illusion...

I must learn to love the self

In so, I will learn to love you...

And what an easy lesson!

You, so fair and lovely,

Lovely as the sun on an idealized stream of thought,

You, who shall snare the dream that eluded me...

I will prop you up

For others broke me

I will hold you close

For they struck me down

I will save you

When others left me to burn,

In a furnace of self-indulgence...

Vivian, lady of the depths…

She who raises the sword and symbol,

Of the highest light—to join the worlds of dreaming, melancholy men…

As you age, and I grey,

I will fight against my broken nature,

To give you peace…

A peace that I will never know—queen of snows,

Ice blue and clean as a frozen breath…

Here, I stand in awe,

Shielded from death…

You touch my cheek, and the honor scars me,

In this silent, sacred place,

Heart-to-heart, and face-to-face…

Vivian—saint of children,

Angel of light.